50 Art of Bread Baking Dishes for Home

By: Kelly Johnson

Table of Contents

- Sourdough bread
- Focaccia
- Ciabatta
- French baguette
- Brioche
- Whole wheat bread
- Multigrain bread
- Pita bread
- Naan
- Rye bread
- Challah
- Pull-apart bread
- Pretzels
- Pizza dough
- Bagels
- Cinnamon rolls
- Sticky buns
- Garlic bread
- Pain de Campagne
- Bâtard
- Pain Complet (Whole wheat French bread)
- Gluten-free bread
- Irish soda bread
- Brioche buns
- Flatbreads
- English muffins
- Lavash
- Coburg
- Pumpernickel
- Anadama bread
- Pain d'épi
- Pain de Mie
- Milk bread
- Croissants
- Pain Viennois

- Pain de Mie
- Pain Poilâne
- Zopf (Swiss braid)
- Hawaiian sweet rolls
- Coburg loaf
- Fougasse
- Kamut bread
- Ezekiel bread
- Panettone
- Stollen
- Lavash
- Pão de queijo (Brazilian cheese bread)
- Sweet potato bread
- Pandoro
- Turmeric and black sesame bread

Sourdough Bread

Ingredients:

- 1 1/2 cups (240g) active sourdough starter
- 1 1/2 cups (375ml) water
- 4 cups (500g) all-purpose flour
- 2 tsp salt

Instructions:

1. In a large bowl, mix sourdough starter and water. Gradually add flour and salt, mixing until a dough forms.
2. Knead the dough on a floured surface for about 10 minutes until smooth.
3. Place the dough in a lightly oiled bowl, cover, and let rise for 4-6 hours or until doubled in size.
4. Punch down the dough, shape it into a loaf, and place it on a baking sheet or in a Dutch oven.
5. Preheat oven to 450°F (230°C) and bake for 30-35 minutes until golden.

Focaccia

Ingredients:

- 3 cups (375g) all-purpose flour
- 1 tsp salt
- 1 tsp sugar
- 1 packet (7g) active dry yeast
- 1 1/4 cups (310ml) warm water
- 1/4 cup (60ml) olive oil, plus extra for drizzling
- Fresh rosemary (optional)
- Coarse sea salt

Instructions:

1. In a bowl, dissolve sugar and yeast in warm water. Let sit for 5-10 minutes until foamy.
2. Mix flour and salt, then add yeast mixture and 1/4 cup olive oil. Knead until smooth.
3. Let rise for 1-2 hours until doubled in size.
4. Preheat oven to 400°F (200°C). Grease a baking sheet and transfer dough.
5. Press your fingers into the dough to create dimples, drizzle with olive oil, sprinkle with rosemary and sea salt.
6. Bake for 20-25 minutes until golden.

Ciabatta

Ingredients:

- 3 cups (375g) all-purpose flour
- 1 tsp salt
- 1 tsp sugar
- 1 packet (7g) active dry yeast
- 1 1/2 cups (375ml) warm water
- 2 tbsp olive oil

Instructions:

1. In a bowl, combine yeast, sugar, and warm water. Let sit for 5-10 minutes until bubbly.
2. Add flour and salt to the yeast mixture, then knead for 10 minutes until smooth.
3. Let rise in an oiled bowl, covered, for 1-2 hours until doubled.
4. Preheat oven to 450°F (230°C).
5. Gently deflate the dough, shape into a rustic loaf, and bake for 25-30 minutes until golden.

French Baguette

Ingredients:

- 3 1/2 cups (440g) all-purpose flour
- 1 tsp salt
- 1 tsp sugar
- 1 packet (7g) active dry yeast
- 1 1/4 cups (310ml) warm water
- 1 tbsp olive oil (optional)

Instructions:

1. Mix sugar, yeast, and warm water in a bowl. Let sit for 5-10 minutes until bubbly.
2. Add flour and salt, then knead for about 10 minutes.
3. Let dough rise for 1-2 hours until doubled in size.
4. Preheat oven to 475°F (245°C).
5. Shape dough into long baguettes, place on a baking sheet, and let rise for another 30 minutes.
6. Slash the top with a sharp knife, then bake for 20-25 minutes until golden.

Brioche

Ingredients:

- 1 1/2 cups (180g) all-purpose flour
- 1/2 cup (60g) sugar
- 1 tsp salt
- 1 packet (7g) active dry yeast
- 1/2 cup (120ml) milk, warm
- 4 large eggs
- 1/2 cup (115g) butter, softened

Instructions:

1. Dissolve sugar and yeast in warm milk, then let sit for 5-10 minutes.
2. In a large bowl, mix flour, salt, and eggs. Add yeast mixture and knead for 10-12 minutes.
3. Gradually add butter, kneading until dough is smooth.
4. Let rise for 1-2 hours until doubled in size.
5. Preheat oven to 350°F (180°C). Grease a loaf pan and transfer dough.
6. Bake for 25-30 minutes until golden.

Whole Wheat Bread

Ingredients:

- 3 cups (375g) whole wheat flour
- 1 1/2 cups (375ml) warm water
- 1 tbsp honey
- 1 packet (7g) active dry yeast
- 1 tbsp olive oil
- 1 tsp salt

Instructions:

1. Dissolve honey and yeast in warm water, let sit for 5-10 minutes.
2. In a large bowl, mix whole wheat flour and salt. Add yeast mixture and olive oil.
3. Knead for 10 minutes, then let rise for 1-2 hours until doubled.
4. Preheat oven to 375°F (190°C). Grease a loaf pan and shape dough into a loaf.
5. Bake for 30-35 minutes until golden and hollow when tapped.

Multigrain Bread

Ingredients:

- 2 cups (250g) all-purpose flour
- 1 cup (125g) whole wheat flour
- 1/2 cup (60g) rolled oats
- 1/4 cup (30g) sunflower seeds
- 1/4 cup (30g) flaxseeds
- 1 tsp salt
- 1 tbsp sugar
- 1 packet (7g) active dry yeast
- 1 1/2 cups (375ml) warm water

Instructions:

1. Mix sugar, yeast, and warm water in a bowl. Let sit for 5-10 minutes.
2. Combine flours, oats, seeds, and salt in a large bowl.
3. Add yeast mixture and knead for 10 minutes until smooth.
4. Let rise for 1-2 hours until doubled in size.
5. Preheat oven to 375°F (190°C). Grease a loaf pan and shape dough into a loaf.
6. Bake for 30-35 minutes until golden and hollow when tapped.

Pita Bread

Ingredients:

- 2 1/2 cups (320g) all-purpose flour
- 1 tsp salt
- 1 tsp sugar
- 1 packet (7g) active dry yeast
- 1 1/4 cups (310ml) warm water
- 2 tbsp olive oil

Instructions:

1. Dissolve sugar and yeast in warm water. Let sit for 5-10 minutes.
2. Add flour and salt, then knead for 8-10 minutes until smooth.
3. Let rise for 1-2 hours until doubled.
4. Preheat oven to 475°F (245°C). Place a baking sheet in the oven.
5. Shape dough into balls, roll out, and bake for 5-7 minutes.

Naan

Ingredients:

- 3 cups (375g) all-purpose flour
- 1 tsp salt
- 1 tsp sugar
- 1 packet (7g) active dry yeast
- 1/2 cup (120ml) warm water
- 1/2 cup (120g) plain yogurt
- 2 tbsp olive oil

Instructions:

1. Mix sugar, yeast, and warm water. Let sit for 5-10 minutes.
2. Combine flour, salt, and sugar. Add yeast mixture, yogurt, and olive oil.
3. Knead for 10 minutes, then let rise for 1-2 hours.
4. Preheat a skillet over medium-high heat.
5. Roll dough into rounds, then cook for 2-3 minutes on each side until golden.

Rye Bread

Ingredients:

- 2 cups (250g) rye flour
- 2 cups (250g) all-purpose flour
- 1 tsp salt
- 1 packet (7g) active dry yeast
- 1 1/2 cups (375ml) warm water
- 1 tbsp molasses

Instructions:

1. Dissolve yeast and molasses in warm water. Let sit for 5-10 minutes.
2. Mix rye and all-purpose flours with salt. Add yeast mixture and knead for 10 minutes.
3. Let rise for 1-2 hours until doubled.
4. Preheat oven to 375°F (190°C). Grease a loaf pan and transfer dough.
5. Bake for 30-35 minutes until golden.

Challah

Ingredients:

- 4 cups (500g) all-purpose flour
- 1 tsp salt
- 1/4 cup (50g) sugar
- 1 packet (7g) active dry yeast
- 1 1/4 cups (310ml) warm water
- 2 tbsp olive oil
- 2 large eggs
- 1 egg (for egg wash)

Instructions:

1. Dissolve sugar and yeast in warm water. Let sit for 5-10 minutes.
2. Add flour, salt, eggs, and olive oil to yeast mixture. Knead for 10 minutes until smooth.
3. Let rise for 1-2 hours until doubled.
4. Preheat oven to 350°F (180°C).
5. Braid dough, place on a baking sheet, and let rise for 30 minutes.
6. Brush with egg wash and bake for 25-30 minutes until golden.

Pull-Apart Bread

Ingredients:

- 3 cups (375g) all-purpose flour
- 1 packet (7g) active dry yeast
- 1/4 cup (50g) sugar
- 1 tsp salt
- 1/2 cup (120ml) warm milk
- 1/2 cup (115g) butter, melted
- 2 large eggs

Instructions:

1. In a bowl, mix warm milk, sugar, and yeast. Let sit for 5-10 minutes until bubbly.
2. Add melted butter, eggs, salt, and flour, then knead until smooth.
3. Let dough rise for 1-2 hours until doubled.
4. Roll dough into small balls, arrange them in a greased baking dish, and let rise for another 30 minutes.
5. Preheat oven to 350°F (180°C). Bake for 25-30 minutes until golden.

Pretzels

Ingredients:

- 2 1/4 cups (280g) all-purpose flour
- 1 packet (7g) active dry yeast
- 1 tsp salt
- 1 cup (240ml) warm water
- 1 tbsp sugar
- 1 tbsp baking soda
- 1 egg (for egg wash)

Instructions:

1. Dissolve sugar and yeast in warm water. Let sit for 5-10 minutes until foamy.
2. Add flour and salt to the yeast mixture, knead for 8-10 minutes until smooth.
3. Let dough rise for 1-1.5 hours until doubled.
4. Preheat oven to 450°F (230°C). Boil a pot of water and add baking soda.
5. Shape dough into pretzels, dip each in the boiling water for 30 seconds, then place on a baking sheet.
6. Brush with egg wash and bake for 12-15 minutes until golden.

Pizza Dough

Ingredients:

- 3 1/2 cups (440g) all-purpose flour
- 1 packet (7g) active dry yeast
- 1 tsp salt
- 1 tsp sugar
- 1 1/2 cups (375ml) warm water
- 2 tbsp olive oil

Instructions:

1. Dissolve sugar and yeast in warm water. Let sit for 5-10 minutes until bubbly.
2. Add flour, salt, and olive oil to the yeast mixture. Knead for 8-10 minutes until smooth.
3. Let dough rise for 1-2 hours until doubled in size.
4. Preheat oven to 475°F (245°C). Roll dough into desired shape and bake with toppings for 10-12 minutes.

Bagels

Ingredients:

- 4 cups (500g) all-purpose flour
- 1 packet (7g) active dry yeast
- 1 tsp salt
- 1 tbsp sugar
- 1 1/2 cups (375ml) warm water
- 1 tbsp honey (for boiling)

Instructions:

1. Dissolve sugar and yeast in warm water. Let sit for 5-10 minutes.
2. Add flour and salt, knead for 10 minutes until smooth.
3. Let dough rise for 1-1.5 hours until doubled.
4. Preheat oven to 425°F (220°C).
5. Boil water with honey, then shape dough into bagels and boil for 1-2 minutes per side.
6. Bake for 20-25 minutes until golden.

Cinnamon Rolls

Ingredients:

For the dough:

- 3 cups (375g) all-purpose flour
- 1 packet (7g) active dry yeast
- 1/4 cup (50g) sugar
- 1 tsp salt
- 1 cup (240ml) warm milk
- 1/4 cup (60g) butter, melted
- 2 large eggs

For the filling:

- 1/2 cup (115g) butter, softened
- 1 cup (200g) brown sugar
- 1 tbsp ground cinnamon

For the icing:

- 1/2 cup (120g) powdered sugar
- 2 tbsp milk
- 1/4 tsp vanilla extract

Instructions:

1. Dissolve sugar and yeast in warm milk, let sit for 5-10 minutes.
2. Add melted butter, eggs, salt, and flour, then knead until smooth.
3. Let dough rise for 1-1.5 hours until doubled.
4. Roll dough into a rectangle, spread with butter, then sprinkle with brown sugar and cinnamon.
5. Roll up dough, slice into rolls, and place on a greased baking dish. Let rise for 30-45 minutes.
6. Preheat oven to 350°F (180°C) and bake for 20-25 minutes.
7. Mix icing ingredients and drizzle over warm rolls.

Sticky Buns

Ingredients:

For the dough:

- 3 cups (375g) all-purpose flour
- 1 packet (7g) active dry yeast
- 1/4 cup (50g) sugar
- 1 tsp salt
- 1/2 cup (120ml) warm milk
- 1/4 cup (60g) butter, melted
- 2 large eggs

For the filling:

- 1/2 cup (115g) butter, softened
- 1 cup (200g) brown sugar
- 1 tsp cinnamon
- 1 cup (150g) chopped pecans

For the glaze:

- 1/2 cup (120g) butter
- 1 cup (200g) brown sugar
- 2 tbsp heavy cream

Instructions:

1. Dissolve sugar and yeast in warm milk, let sit for 5-10 minutes.
2. Add melted butter, eggs, salt, and flour, then knead until smooth.
3. Let dough rise for 1-1.5 hours.
4. Roll out dough, spread with butter, and sprinkle with brown sugar, cinnamon, and chopped pecans.
5. Roll up dough, slice into rolls, and place in a greased baking dish. Let rise for 30-45 minutes.
6. Preheat oven to 350°F (180°C) and bake for 20-25 minutes.
7. Melt butter, brown sugar, and heavy cream in a saucepan, then drizzle over warm buns.

Garlic Bread

Ingredients:

- 1 loaf French or Italian bread
- 1/2 cup (115g) butter, softened
- 3-4 cloves garlic, minced
- 1 tbsp fresh parsley, chopped
- 1/4 tsp salt

Instructions:

1. Preheat oven to 375°F (190°C).
2. Slice bread in half lengthwise.
3. Mix softened butter, garlic, parsley, and salt. Spread on cut sides of bread.
4. Wrap in foil and bake for 10-12 minutes.
5. Optionally, open foil and bake for an additional 5 minutes for a crispier crust.

Pain de Campagne (French Country Bread)

Ingredients:

- 3 cups (375g) all-purpose flour
- 1 1/2 cups (375ml) warm water
- 1 tsp salt
- 1 packet (7g) active dry yeast
- 1 tbsp olive oil

Instructions:

1. Dissolve yeast and salt in warm water, let sit for 5-10 minutes.
2. Add flour and olive oil, then knead for 10 minutes.
3. Let dough rise for 1-1.5 hours until doubled.
4. Preheat oven to 450°F (230°C).
5. Shape dough into a round loaf, place on a baking sheet, and let rise for 30 minutes.
6. Bake for 30-35 minutes until golden and hollow when tapped.

Bâtard

Ingredients:

- 3 cups (375g) all-purpose flour
- 1 1/2 cups (375ml) warm water
- 1 tsp salt
- 1 packet (7g) active dry yeast
- 1 tbsp olive oil

Instructions:

1. Dissolve yeast and salt in warm water. Let sit for 5-10 minutes.
2. Add flour and olive oil, knead for 10 minutes until smooth.
3. Let dough rise for 1-1.5 hours.
4. Preheat oven to 450°F (230°C). Shape dough into a long loaf.
5. Bake for 20-25 minutes until golden and hollow when tapped.

Pain Complet (Whole Wheat French Bread)

Ingredients:

- 2 1/2 cups (310g) whole wheat flour
- 1 1/2 cups (375ml) warm water
- 1 tsp salt
- 1 packet (7g) active dry yeast
- 1 tbsp olive oil

Instructions:

1. Dissolve yeast and salt in warm water. Let sit for 5-10 minutes.
2. Add flour and olive oil, knead for 10 minutes.
3. Let dough rise for 1-1.5 hours.
4. Preheat oven to 425°F (220°C). Shape dough into a round loaf and place on a baking sheet.
5. Bake for 25-30 minutes until golden and hollow when tapped.

Gluten-Free Bread

Ingredients:

- 2 1/2 cups (300g) gluten-free all-purpose flour
- 1 tsp salt
- 1 tbsp sugar
- 1 packet (7g) active dry yeast
- 1 1/2 cups (375ml) warm water
- 1/4 cup (60ml) olive oil
- 1 tsp vinegar
- 2 large eggs

Instructions:

1. Dissolve sugar and yeast in warm water, let sit for 5-10 minutes until bubbly.
2. In a large bowl, mix gluten-free flour and salt. Add yeast mixture, olive oil, vinegar, and eggs.
3. Mix until smooth, then pour into a greased loaf pan.
4. Let rise for 1-1.5 hours until doubled.
5. Preheat oven to 375°F (190°C) and bake for 30-35 minutes until golden and hollow when tapped.

Irish Soda Bread

Ingredients:

- 4 cups (500g) all-purpose flour
- 1 tsp salt
- 1 tsp baking soda
- 1 1/2 cups (375ml) buttermilk

Instructions:

1. Preheat oven to 425°F (220°C). Grease a baking sheet.
2. In a bowl, mix flour, salt, and baking soda.
3. Add buttermilk and stir to form a dough.
4. Turn out onto a floured surface and shape into a round loaf.
5. Score the top with an "X" and bake for 35-40 minutes until golden.

Brioche Buns

Ingredients:

- 3 cups (375g) all-purpose flour
- 1/4 cup (50g) sugar
- 1 packet (7g) active dry yeast
- 1/2 cup (120ml) warm milk
- 1/2 cup (115g) butter, softened
- 3 large eggs
- 1 tsp salt

Instructions:

1. Dissolve sugar and yeast in warm milk, let sit for 5-10 minutes.
2. Add flour, eggs, butter, and salt to the yeast mixture. Knead for 10 minutes until smooth.
3. Let dough rise for 1-2 hours until doubled.
4. Preheat oven to 375°F (190°C).
5. Divide dough into small buns, shape, and place on a baking sheet. Let rise for 30-45 minutes.
6. Bake for 15-20 minutes until golden.

Flatbreads

Ingredients:

- 2 cups (250g) all-purpose flour
- 1 tsp salt
- 1 tsp baking powder
- 1 tbsp olive oil
- 3/4 cup (180ml) warm water

Instructions:

1. In a bowl, mix flour, salt, and baking powder.
2. Add olive oil and warm water, then knead for 5-7 minutes until smooth.
3. Divide dough into small portions and roll each into a thin circle.
4. Heat a skillet over medium-high heat. Cook flatbreads for 2-3 minutes on each side until lightly browned.

English Muffins

Ingredients:

- 3 cups (375g) all-purpose flour
- 1 packet (7g) active dry yeast
- 1/2 tsp salt
- 1 tsp sugar
- 1/2 cup (120ml) warm milk
- 1/4 cup (60ml) water
- 1 tbsp butter, softened

Instructions:

1. Dissolve sugar and yeast in warm milk and water, let sit for 5-10 minutes.
2. Mix flour and salt, then add yeast mixture and butter.
3. Knead for 8-10 minutes, then let dough rise for 1-1.5 hours until doubled.
4. Preheat a griddle or skillet over medium heat.
5. Roll out dough and cut into circles. Cook muffins for 5-7 minutes on each side until golden.

Lavash

Ingredients:

- 2 cups (250g) all-purpose flour
- 1 tsp salt
- 1 tsp sugar
- 1 packet (7g) active dry yeast
- 3/4 cup (180ml) warm water
- 2 tbsp olive oil

Instructions:

1. Dissolve sugar and yeast in warm water, let sit for 5-10 minutes.
2. In a bowl, mix flour and salt, then add yeast mixture and olive oil.
3. Knead for 8-10 minutes until smooth, then let rise for 1 hour.
4. Preheat oven to 475°F (245°C).
5. Roll dough into thin rounds and bake on a baking sheet for 5-7 minutes until lightly browned.

Coburg

Ingredients:

- 3 1/2 cups (440g) all-purpose flour
- 1 tsp salt
- 1 packet (7g) active dry yeast
- 1 1/4 cups (310ml) warm water
- 1 tbsp sugar
- 1 tbsp olive oil

Instructions:

1. Dissolve sugar and yeast in warm water, let sit for 5-10 minutes.
2. Mix flour and salt, then add yeast mixture and olive oil. Knead for 10 minutes.
3. Let dough rise for 1-1.5 hours until doubled.
4. Preheat oven to 400°F (200°C).
5. Shape dough into a round loaf and bake for 25-30 minutes until golden and hollow when tapped.

Pumpernickel

Ingredients:

- 2 cups (250g) whole rye flour
- 2 cups (250g) all-purpose flour
- 1 packet (7g) active dry yeast
- 1 tsp salt
- 1 tbsp molasses
- 1 1/2 cups (375ml) warm water

Instructions:

1. Dissolve molasses and yeast in warm water, let sit for 5-10 minutes.
2. Mix rye flour, all-purpose flour, and salt. Add yeast mixture and knead for 8-10 minutes.
3. Let dough rise for 1-1.5 hours until doubled.
4. Preheat oven to 375°F (190°C).
5. Shape dough into a loaf and bake for 30-35 minutes until golden.

Anadama Bread

Ingredients:

- 1 cup (240ml) warm water
- 1 packet (7g) active dry yeast
- 1/4 cup (50g) molasses
- 1 cup (125g) cornmeal
- 2 cups (250g) all-purpose flour
- 1 tsp salt
- 1 tbsp butter, softened

Instructions:

1. Dissolve yeast and molasses in warm water, let sit for 5-10 minutes.
2. Stir in cornmeal, flour, and salt. Knead for 8-10 minutes.
3. Let dough rise for 1-1.5 hours.
4. Preheat oven to 375°F (190°C).
5. Shape dough into a loaf and bake for 25-30 minutes until golden.

Pain d'épi

Ingredients:

- 4 cups (500g) all-purpose flour
- 1 1/2 cups (375ml) warm water
- 1 packet (7g) active dry yeast
- 1 tsp salt
- 1 tbsp olive oil

Instructions:

1. Dissolve yeast and salt in warm water, let sit for 5-10 minutes.
2. Mix flour and yeast mixture, then knead for 10 minutes.
3. Let dough rise for 1-1.5 hours until doubled.
4. Preheat oven to 450°F (230°C).
5. Shape dough into a long baguette or a decorative spike shape, and bake for 25-30 minutes until golden.

Pain de Mie

Ingredients:

- 3 cups (375g) all-purpose flour
- 1 tsp salt
- 1 tbsp sugar
- 1 packet (7g) active dry yeast
- 1 1/4 cups (310ml) warm milk
- 1 tbsp butter, softened

Instructions:

1. Dissolve sugar and yeast in warm milk, let sit for 5-10 minutes.
2. Mix flour and salt, add yeast mixture and softened butter.
3. Knead dough for 10 minutes until smooth.
4. Let rise for 1-1.5 hours until doubled in size.
5. Preheat oven to 375°F (190°C).
6. Shape dough into a loaf and bake for 25-30 minutes until golden.

Milk Bread

Ingredients:

- 3 cups (375g) all-purpose flour
- 1 packet (7g) active dry yeast
- 1 tsp salt
- 1/4 cup (50g) sugar
- 1/2 cup (120ml) milk
- 1/2 cup (120ml) warm water
- 1/4 cup (60g) butter, softened

Instructions:

1. Dissolve sugar and yeast in warm water, let sit for 5-10 minutes.
2. Warm the milk, then add it to the yeast mixture along with salt and butter.
3. Gradually add flour and knead for 10 minutes until smooth.
4. Let dough rise for 1-1.5 hours until doubled.
5. Preheat oven to 350°F (180°C). Grease a loaf pan.
6. Shape dough into a loaf and bake for 30-35 minutes until golden.

Croissants

Ingredients:

- 2 1/2 cups (320g) all-purpose flour
- 1 tbsp sugar
- 1 tsp salt
- 1 packet (7g) active dry yeast
- 1 1/4 cups (310ml) warm milk
- 1 cup (225g) cold butter, cubed
- 1 egg (for egg wash)

Instructions:

1. Dissolve yeast and sugar in warm milk, let sit for 5-10 minutes.
2. Mix flour and salt, then add the yeast mixture. Knead for 8-10 minutes until smooth.
3. Let dough rise for 1 hour, then refrigerate for 1-2 hours.
4. Roll dough into a rectangle, fold in the cold butter, then roll out and fold again (lamination process).
5. Let dough rest for 30 minutes, repeat folding process 2 more times.
6. Shape dough into croissants, brush with egg wash, and bake at 375°F (190°C) for 12-15 minutes until golden.

Pain Viennois

Ingredients:

- 2 1/2 cups (310g) all-purpose flour
- 1 packet (7g) active dry yeast
- 1/4 cup (50g) sugar
- 1 tsp salt
- 1 cup (240ml) milk
- 1/4 cup (60g) butter, softened
- 1 egg

Instructions:

1. Dissolve yeast and sugar in warm milk, let sit for 5-10 minutes.
2. Add flour, salt, and softened butter to the yeast mixture, then knead for 8-10 minutes.
3. Let dough rise for 1-1.5 hours.
4. Preheat oven to 375°F (190°C).
5. Shape dough into a loaf, place in a greased pan, and let rise for 30 minutes.
6. Brush with beaten egg and bake for 25-30 minutes until golden.

Pain de Mie

Ingredients:

- 3 cups (375g) all-purpose flour
- 1 tsp salt
- 1 tbsp sugar
- 1 packet (7g) active dry yeast
- 1 1/4 cups (310ml) warm milk
- 1 tbsp butter, softened

Instructions:

1. Dissolve sugar and yeast in warm milk, let sit for 5-10 minutes until bubbly.
2. Mix flour and salt, add yeast mixture and softened butter.
3. Knead dough for 10 minutes until smooth and elastic.
4. Let dough rise for 1-1.5 hours until doubled in size.
5. Preheat oven to 375°F (190°C).
6. Grease a loaf pan and shape dough into a loaf, place it in the pan. Let rise for another 30 minutes.
7. Bake for 25-30 minutes until golden brown and hollow when tapped on top.
8. Let cool before slicing.

Pain Poilâne

Ingredients:

- 3 cups (375g) all-purpose flour
- 1 1/2 cups (375ml) warm water
- 1 packet (7g) active dry yeast
- 1 tsp salt
- 1 tbsp honey
- 1/4 cup (60g) sourdough starter (optional)

Instructions:

1. Dissolve yeast, honey, and sourdough starter (if using) in warm water. Let sit for 5-10 minutes.
2. Add flour and salt, knead for 10 minutes until smooth.
3. Let dough rise for 1-2 hours until doubled in size.
4. Preheat oven to 450°F (230°C).
5. Shape dough into a round boule and bake on a baking sheet for 35-40 minutes until golden and hollow when tapped.

Zopf (Swiss Braid)

Ingredients:

- 3 cups (375g) all-purpose flour
- 1 packet (7g) active dry yeast
- 1/2 tsp salt
- 1/4 cup (50g) sugar
- 1/2 cup (120ml) milk
- 1/2 cup (115g) butter, softened
- 1 egg (for egg wash)

Instructions:

1. Dissolve yeast and sugar in warm milk, let sit for 5-10 minutes.
2. Mix flour, salt, and the yeast mixture. Add butter and knead for 10 minutes until smooth.
3. Let dough rise for 1-1.5 hours.
4. Preheat oven to 375°F (190°C).
5. Divide dough into 3 parts, braid them, and place on a baking sheet.
6. Let rise for 30 minutes, then brush with egg wash.
7. Bake for 20-25 minutes until golden.

Hawaiian Sweet Rolls

Ingredients:

- 3 cups (375g) all-purpose flour
- 1 packet (7g) active dry yeast
- 1/4 cup (50g) sugar
- 1 tsp salt
- 1/2 cup (120ml) pineapple juice
- 1/4 cup (60g) butter, softened
- 1 egg

Instructions:

1. Dissolve yeast and sugar in warm pineapple juice, let sit for 5-10 minutes.
2. Add flour, salt, butter, and egg. Knead for 10 minutes until smooth.
3. Let dough rise for 1-1.5 hours.
4. Preheat oven to 350°F (180°C). Grease a baking dish.
5. Shape dough into small rolls, place in the dish, and let rise for 30-45 minutes.
6. Bake for 15-20 minutes until golden.

Coburg Loaf

Ingredients:

- 3 1/2 cups (440g) all-purpose flour
- 1 tsp salt
- 1 packet (7g) active dry yeast
- 1 1/4 cups (310ml) warm water
- 1 tbsp sugar
- 1 tbsp olive oil

Instructions:

1. Dissolve sugar and yeast in warm water, let sit for 5-10 minutes.
2. Mix flour and salt, then add yeast mixture and olive oil. Knead for 10 minutes.
3. Let dough rise for 1-1.5 hours until doubled.
4. Preheat oven to 400°F (200°C).
5. Shape dough into a round loaf and bake for 25-30 minutes until golden and hollow when tapped.

Fougasse

Ingredients:

- 3 cups (375g) all-purpose flour
- 1 packet (7g) active dry yeast
- 1 tsp salt
- 1/2 tsp sugar
- 1 cup (240ml) warm water
- 1/4 cup (60ml) olive oil
- Fresh rosemary (optional)

Instructions:

1. Dissolve sugar and yeast in warm water, let sit for 5-10 minutes.
2. Add flour, salt, and olive oil, then knead for 8-10 minutes.
3. Let dough rise for 1-1.5 hours.
4. Preheat oven to 375°F (190°C).
5. Roll dough into a flat oval, shape, and cut slits in the top.
6. Brush with olive oil, sprinkle with rosemary, and bake for 15-20 minutes until golden.

Kamut Bread

Ingredients:

- 3 cups (375g) kamut flour
- 1 packet (7g) active dry yeast
- 1 tsp salt
- 1/4 cup (50g) honey
- 1 1/4 cups (310ml) warm water
- 2 tbsp olive oil

Instructions:

1. Dissolve honey and yeast in warm water, let sit for 5-10 minutes.
2. Mix kamut flour and salt, then add yeast mixture and olive oil. Knead for 10 minutes until smooth.
3. Let dough rise for 1-1.5 hours until doubled in size.
4. Preheat oven to 375°F (190°C). Grease a loaf pan.
5. Shape dough into a loaf and bake for 30-35 minutes until golden.

Ezekiel Bread

Ingredients:

- 1 cup (150g) whole wheat berries
- 1 cup (150g) barley
- 1 cup (150g) spelt berries
- 1/2 cup (75g) lentils
- 1 packet (7g) active dry yeast
- 1 tbsp honey
- 1 1/2 cups (375ml) warm water
- 1 tsp salt
- 3 cups (375g) all-purpose flour

Instructions:

1. Soak wheat berries, barley, spelt berries, and lentils in water overnight.
2. The next day, drain and blend the grains and lentils in a food processor until they form a dough-like consistency.
3. Dissolve yeast and honey in warm water, and let sit for 5-10 minutes.
4. Add the soaked mixture to the yeast mixture and knead in salt and flour.
5. Let dough rise for 1-2 hours, then shape into a loaf and let rise for another 30 minutes.
6. Preheat oven to 375°F (190°C).
7. Bake for 30-35 minutes until golden and hollow when tapped.

Panettone

Ingredients:

- 4 cups (500g) all-purpose flour
- 1 packet (7g) active dry yeast
- 1 tsp salt
- 1/2 cup (100g) sugar
- 1/2 cup (120ml) warm milk
- 1/2 cup (115g) butter, softened
- 4 large eggs
- 1 tsp vanilla extract
- 1/2 cup (75g) mixed dried fruit
- 1/2 cup (75g) candied peel
- 1/4 cup (50g) chopped almonds

Instructions:

1. Dissolve yeast and sugar in warm milk, let sit for 5-10 minutes.
2. In a large bowl, mix flour, salt, and eggs. Add yeast mixture, butter, and vanilla, knead for 10 minutes.
3. Let dough rise for 2-3 hours until doubled.
4. Stir in dried fruit, candied peel, and almonds.
5. Preheat oven to 350°F (180°C).
6. Shape dough into a round loaf and place in a panettone mold. Let rise for 30-60 minutes.
7. Bake for 35-40 minutes until golden and hollow when tapped.

Stollen

Ingredients:

- 3 cups (375g) all-purpose flour
- 1 packet (7g) active dry yeast
- 1/2 cup (100g) sugar
- 1 tsp salt
- 1/2 tsp ground cinnamon
- 1/2 tsp ground nutmeg
- 1/2 cup (120ml) milk
- 1/2 cup (115g) butter, softened
- 2 large eggs
- 1/2 cup (75g) dried fruit (raisins, currants, etc.)
- 1/4 cup (50g) chopped almonds
- 1/4 cup (50g) candied peel
- 1 tbsp brandy or rum

Instructions:

1. Dissolve sugar and yeast in warm milk, let sit for 5-10 minutes.
2. Add flour, salt, cinnamon, and nutmeg. Knead in butter, eggs, and dried fruit.
3. Let dough rise for 1-2 hours.
4. Preheat oven to 350°F (180°C).
5. Shape dough into a loaf and fold it over to resemble a "stollen" shape.
6. Let rise for 30 minutes, then bake for 30-35 minutes until golden.

Lavash

Ingredients:

- 2 cups (250g) all-purpose flour
- 1/2 tsp salt
- 1 tsp sugar
- 1 packet (7g) active dry yeast
- 3/4 cup (180ml) warm water
- 2 tbsp olive oil

Instructions:

1. Dissolve sugar and yeast in warm water, let sit for 5-10 minutes.
2. Add flour and salt, then knead for 8-10 minutes.
3. Let dough rise for 1 hour.
4. Preheat oven to 475°F (245°C).
5. Roll dough out thinly, place on a baking sheet, and bake for 3-5 minutes until golden and crispy.

Pão de Queijo (Brazilian Cheese Bread)

Ingredients:

- 2 cups (250g) tapioca flour
- 1/2 cup (120ml) milk
- 1/2 cup (115g) butter
- 1 1/2 cups (180g) grated Parmesan cheese
- 1/2 cup (60g) grated mozzarella cheese
- 1 egg
- 1/2 tsp salt

Instructions:

1. Preheat oven to 375°F (190°C). Grease a baking sheet.
2. Heat milk and butter together until butter melts, then pour over tapioca flour. Stir in cheeses, egg, and salt.
3. Mix into a sticky dough and shape into small balls.
4. Place on a baking sheet and bake for 15-20 minutes until puffed and golden.

Sweet Potato Bread

Ingredients:

- 2 cups (250g) all-purpose flour
- 1 packet (7g) active dry yeast
- 1 tsp salt
- 1/4 cup (50g) sugar
- 1/2 cup (120ml) warm milk
- 1/2 cup (120g) mashed sweet potato
- 2 tbsp butter, softened

Instructions:

1. Dissolve sugar and yeast in warm milk, let sit for 5-10 minutes.
2. Add mashed sweet potato, flour, salt, and butter, then knead for 8-10 minutes.
3. Let dough rise for 1-1.5 hours.
4. Preheat oven to 350°F (180°C). Grease a loaf pan.
5. Shape dough into a loaf and bake for 30-35 minutes until golden and hollow when tapped.

Pandoro

Ingredients:

- 4 cups (500g) all-purpose flour
- 1 packet (7g) active dry yeast
- 1 tsp salt
- 1/2 cup (100g) sugar
- 1/2 cup (120ml) warm milk
- 1/2 cup (115g) butter, softened
- 3 large eggs
- 1 tsp vanilla extract

Instructions:

1. Dissolve sugar and yeast in warm milk, let sit for 5-10 minutes.
2. Mix flour, salt, and sugar. Add yeast mixture, butter, eggs, and vanilla. Knead for 10 minutes.
3. Let dough rise for 1-2 hours.
4. Preheat oven to 350°F (180°C). Grease a pandoro mold or a cake pan.
5. Shape dough into a ball, place in the mold, and bake for 30-35 minutes.

Turmeric and Black Sesame Bread

Ingredients:

- 3 cups (375g) all-purpose flour
- 1 packet (7g) active dry yeast
- 1 tsp salt
- 1 tbsp sugar
- 1/2 tsp ground turmeric
- 1/4 cup (60ml) warm water
- 1 tbsp black sesame seeds
- 1/4 cup (60ml) olive oil

Instructions:

1. Dissolve sugar and yeast in warm water, let sit for 5-10 minutes.
2. Add flour, salt, turmeric, and olive oil to the yeast mixture. Knead for 10 minutes until smooth.
3. Let dough rise for 1-1.5 hours.
4. Preheat oven to 375°F (190°C). Shape dough into a loaf, sprinkle with black sesame seeds.
5. Bake for 25-30 minutes until golden and hollow when tapped.

www.ingramcontent.com/pod-product-compliance
Lightning Source LLC
LaVergne TN
LVHW081323060526
838201LV00055B/2423